K. U. SCHNABEL

MODERN TECHNIQUE

OF THE PEDAL

(A PIANO PEDAL STUDY)

Published by

EDIZIONI CURCI

20122 MILANO   GALLERIA DEL CORSO, 4

MODERN TECHNIQUE OF THE PEDAL

(A PIANO PEDAL STUDY)

K. U. SCHNABEL

Pianists have received manifold advice, in books, lectures and lessons, on ways to improve their technique. However, nearly all of this advice refers to the use of the keys; little has been written, said or taught about the use of the pedal. So little, that indeed many pianists do not even realize how they use the pedal themselves. A few rules, sometimes more harmful than helpful, are known to them; the rest is guesswork, instinct, good—or bad—luck.

Even some of the great artists developed their pedal-technique relying upon their ears alone, and certainly, the ear should always be the final judge. But while we can and should learn, *by listening,* which effects are preferable and whether the desired effects are realized or not, the ear alone can not teach us specific methods and means by which these effects are obtained.

The same effect can generally be achieved by many *different* means and methods; some methods will be easy or comparatively easy, some will be very difficult. We believe that it is very difficult to obtain most of the desired effects when using the pedal inadequately or not at all.

There are many ways to acquire a good technique, but some are rather short and others extremely long. We think that the way to acquire a good pedal-technique merely by guessing and experimenting is a long one.

So we would like to offer some suggestions. They might help to shorten the way somewhat.

We shall begin with examples concerning the function of the pedal in holding notes which can not be held with the fingers. Existing material deals mainly with this function. Yet, we believe that the pedal is even more important as an invaluable aid and a decisive influence in the production of sound.

* * * * *

The old system of pedal notation lacks precision in indicating the exact moments when the pedal should be depressed and released. Several modern systems are now in use. Two of these are shown below:

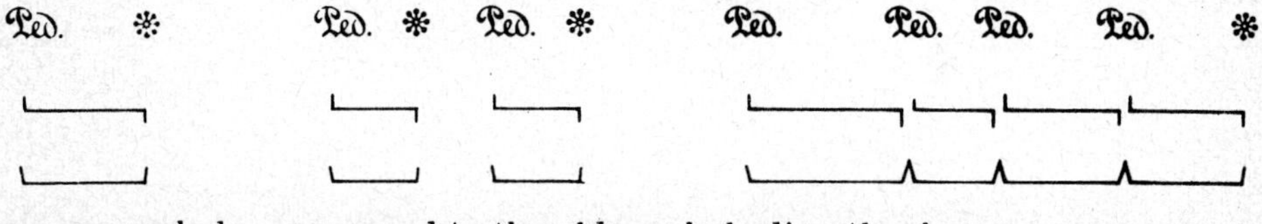

The new symbols correspond to the old symbols directly above.
We shall use the system shown last for our examples.

When playing the following succession of chords, binding with the fingers is impossible, while all degrees of separation or binding can be obtained by means of the pedal:

1) separation: the pedal must be released *before* the next chord is played. This can be done in the last moment

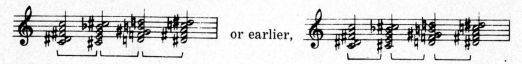

or earlier,

which will determine the degree of separation.

2) connection without any interruption: the pedal must be released *at the moment* when the next chord is played:

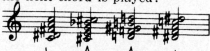

3) intense legato: the pedal should be released immediatly *after* the next chord is played:

Here the degree can be varied, too. However, great care must be taken to avoid the effect of blurring.

An example for separation is found in "Wichtige Begebenheit" ("Important Event") from "Kinderszenen" ("Scenes from Childhood") by Schumann:

Intense legato is recommended for the following bars from Tschaikowsky's b flat minor concerto (first movement):

(Andante non troppo e molto maestoso)

Releasing the pedal and immediately depressing it again is called a change of pedal or pedal change (_____Λ_____). When playing softly and in the middle or higher register, pedal changes can be performed very quickly. When playing in the low register, or f or ff, it may be necessary to perform the changes somewhat more slowly; otherwise the dampers might not stop the vibration of the strings. We suggest marking the difference in the following manner: quick change ____Λ____ ; slower change ___Λ___ .

A simple method, which makes it possible to bind the chords of one hand with the pedal while the other hand plays staccato, is shown in an example from Mendelssohn's "Song without words" opus 62, No. 3:

(Andante maestoso)

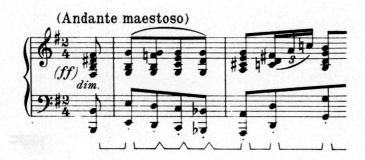

In the last movement of Schubert's B flat major Sonata (opus posth.)

(Allegro ma non troppo)

it is very difficult to bind the right hand melody with the fingers. Binding with the pedal should be much easier and if the pedal changes are performed as indicated here, the staccato notes of the left hand will not be prolonged by the pedal, as it is always released in the moment of playing the staccato.

The staccato and legato indications are, of course, original indications by the composer, as are *all* signs, marks and indications shown in our examples, with exception of pedal markings. Original pedal indications are shown by using the old symbols (℘ed. ✳).

It is very easy to obtain legato by means of the pedal in a slow tempo. The faster the tempo, the more difficult this becomes. But with prolonged practising one can greatly increase the speed at which one is still able to perform such legato. In Mozart's A major Sonata K.V. 331 (first movement, third variation), binding

with the pedal may produce a better legato effect than only binding the upper octave voice with the fingers.

At still greater speeds it becomes impossible to change the pedal exactly with every note, and legato can therefore be obtained only by means of the fingers. However, it may be desirable to use the pedal even at such speeds for other reasons.

This passage from Chopin's c sharp minor Scherzo or

the above octave passage from the second Liszt Concerto (A major) will sound too thin and dry if played without pedal. It is not possible to change pedal on every note. Holding the pedal through groups of 2, 3, 4 notes causes blurring. Depressing the pedal for a short instant on every 3rd, 4th, 6th (etc.) note causes unevenness.

A satisfactory solution may be found in alternately depressing and releasing the pedal as rapidly as possible without trying to make the foot coincide with the hand. The pedal should not be moved all the way up and down, which would be too strenuous and noisy, but only as far as is necessary for the dampers to come in contact with the strings and leave them again, being lifted just far enough so that the strings can vibrate freely. Only a small part of the total possible movement of the pedal lever is needed for this; the rest of the movement is "play" and has no effect upon the sound.

We shall call this rapid motion *"vibrating pedal"* and suggest the following symbol to indicate its use: wwwww

Vibrating pedal will be found very useful in loud scales,

(Beethoven, Concerto in c-minor, first movement)

(Beethoven, Concerto in E flat major, last movement)

particularly chromatic scales,

(Beethoven, Sonata quasi una fantasia, opus 27 No. 2, last movement.)

and all other loud non-harmonic passages where it is impossible to change pedal on every note.

(Mozart, Concerto in d-minor K.V. 466, first movement)

In the following example from Tschaikowsky's b flat minor Concerto (first movement)

it is not impossible to change pedal on every eighth note (quaver), but it is much easier and equally effective to use "vibrating pedal".

* * * * * *

In our first examples, representing a succession of chords, we described the different results obtained by releasing the pedal before, when or after the next chord was played. In every case the pedal was *depressed* again *after* the chord. If the pedal is depressed simultaneously with the chord, some of the sound of the preceding chord will be retained (except if there is an actual pause between the two chords) ; and only if all the notes of both chords belong to the same harmony, will the composite sound be "clean". Otherwise it will be "unclean", slightly or considerably, depending upon the number of dissonant notes and the comparative loudness of the sound which is retained from the previous notes. Because of this we are taught to depress the pedal *after* playing a note or chord when a change of harmony takes place. It is not easy to learn this necessary technique, but once it is acquired it tends to become a habit, is constantly applied, even in places where it is not necessary. Then the pedal is *always* depressed after the notes, while at the moment of playing the pedal is *never* depressed. But this means that we *always* rob ourselves of the aid of the pedal just where its powers for enriching the sound are greatest : at the moment when the hammers strike the strings.

In general, this loss cannot be avoided; but there are many instances where it *is* possible to depress the pedal *while* or *before* the note or chord is played, without any danger of "unclean" sound.

For example, at the beginning of a piece :

(Brahms, Rhapsody in b-minor)

Or after pauses :

(Beethoven, Sonata in d-minor, opus 31, No. 2, 2nd movement)

(Chopin, Scherzo in c sharp minor)

After staccato:

(Beethoven, Sonata opus 26)

At a sudden increase of volume, when the sound retained from preceding notes is so much softer that it will not be heard together with the new notes:

(Chopin, Scherzo in b flat minor)

(Schubert, Sonata in B flat major, opus posth., first movement)

If the increase is very considerable, it may be unnecessary to change the pedal at all:

(Beethoven, Sonata opus 31, No. 2, first movement)

(Allegro assai)

(Beethoven, Sonata opus 57, first movement)

(Allegro assai)

(Beethoven, Sonata opus 57, first movement)

Similarly after a long note:

(Presto)

(Beethoven, Sonata opus 10, No. 3, first movement)

The manner of changing the pedal which was shown earlier, for the purpose of intense legato, also avoids the lack of pedal at the moment of playing:

(Presto con fuoco)
(Meno mosso)

(Chopin, Scherzo in c sharp minor)

12

(Moderato)

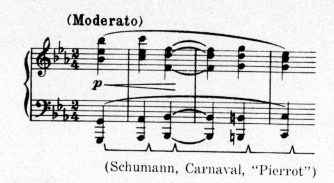

(Schumann, Carnaval, "Pierrot")

(Andante con moto)

(Chopin, Ballade in f minor)

Whenever an upbeat consists only of such notes which are contained in the following harmony, the pedal can be depressed on the upbeat and need not be changed on the beat (except where separation is wanted):

(Sehr rasch)

(Schumann, "Aufschwung"—"Soaring")

It should seem unnecessary to show this and the following examples, but like the habit of *always* depressing the pedal after playing, also the habit of changing pedal on all main beats is widespread.

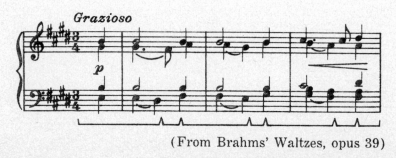

(From Brahms' Waltzes, opus 39)

(From Schumann's Carnaval, "Chiarina")

(Brahms, Sonata opus 5, fourth movement)

This might be recommendable also in cases like the following:

(Schumann, "Papillons")

For "arpeggi" like those at the beginning of the second movement of Schumann's C-major Phantasie (op. 17)

we suggest the following execution:

If the bass-note is played *on* the beat, the pedal will retain the sound of the bass but not any of the previous harmony.

A similar execution is possible in Brahms' Concerto in B flat major:

(Allegro non troppo)

If the bass is played *before* the beat, a slight blurring cannot be avoided. We feel however, that this is preferable to losing the sound of the bass.

* * * * * *

So far we have only discussed the two conventional positions of the pedal: "depressed" and "released". When the pedal is depressed the dampers are removed from the strings and the strings can vibrate freely. When the pedal is released, the dampers rest on the strings and stop their vibrations completely. It is possible, however, to employ the pedal also in *intermediate positions*. When the pedal is kept in an intermediate position, the dampers will allow the strings to vibrate to some extent but will prevent the strings from vibrating freely. Thus a tone will be heard in full strength while the key is held down. When the key is released, the volume will be reduced but some sound remains. We shall use the German word *"Nachklang"* when referring to this remainder of sound. The volume of the "Nachklang" depends upon the position of the dampers. Scarcely any "Nachklang" remains when the dampers are nearly touching the strings, while practically the full volume of sound remains when the dampers are almost completely removed from the strings. All gradations can be obtained by moving the pedal between these two positions.

There are very many instances where the use of intermediate pedal positions can be of great advantage, improving the quality of sound and enlarging its variety.

Let us first consider those places where it would seem inadvisable to use *any* pedal.

(Mozart, Concerto in A-major, K.V. 488, first movement)

Here (as in the examples shown for the use of vibrating pedal) it would be impossible to change pedal on every note. Holding the pedal for more than one note will result in blurring, while alternate depressing and releasing will cause unevenness. Vibrating pedal, which lends itself so well to loud passages, would create too much heaviness here. Yet, when playing without pedal, it will be very difficult to avoid dry and dull sound, even though an excellent legato can be obtained with the fingers.

An intermediate position of the pedal will be helpful here. Of course, for a passage of this nature, only the slightest amount of "Nachklang" should be present—so slight that no blurring whatsoever occurs when the pedal is kept in this position while scales are played or while harmonies change. We shall call this minimum of "Nachklang" "1/4 pedal." Its only effect is to brighten the sound. Pedal changes are not required for "1/4 pedal." It can be used for all medium and high speed scales and non-harmonic passages in *pp* , *p* and *mf* .

We suggest the use of the following symbol to mark "1/4 pedal":

Some examples, where "1/4 pedal" is recommendable, follow:

(Beethoven, Concerto in E flat major, first movement)

(Presto)

(Mendelssohn, "Spinning Song", from "Songs without words", opus 67, No. 4)

(Allegro)

(Beethoven, Sonata opus 81A "Les Adieux," first movement)

(Allegro)

(Beethoven, Concerto in E flat major, first movement)

Also staccato scales and passages can be played with "¼ pedal":

(Allegretto vivace)

(Beethoven, Sonata opus 31, No. 3, 2nd movement)

(Tschaikowsky, Concerto in b-flat minor, 2nd movement)

(From Mendelssohn's "Spinning Song", "Songs without words" opus 67, No. 4)

"¼ pedal" will enrich the sound of the low register:

(Weber, Sonata in e-minor, first movement)

(Beethoven, Sonata opus 81A, "Les Adieux," first movement)

It should be pointed out here that ¼ pedal does *not* indicate a specific position of the pedal. Like the other "intermediate pedals" which are explained below, it indicates *a certain amount of "Nachklang"*. The position of the pedal which produces this amount of Nachklang will vary from one piano to another and may even vary on the same piano under different acoustical conditions.

If the amount of Nachklang is increased by lifting the dampers slightly, an effect is created which we shall call *"1/2 pedal"*. *"½ pedal"* would cause blurring if the pedal were held in this position while scales are played or during a change of harmony, but it will not give the impression that a note is being held after the key is released. Allowing more vibration and resonance, it is an even greater aid to sound than *"¼ pedal"*.

As a means of marking *"½ pedal"*, we suggest the following method:

It will be noted that pedal changes are indicated in the usual manner. The meaning of a pedal change while using *"½ pedal"* is, of course, that the *"½ pedal"* should be released at that instant and a new *"½ pedal"* taken immediately afterwards.

"½ pedal" is particularly useful in harmonic passages where transparency and clarity are desired:

(Beethoven, Concerto in E flat major, first movement)

or in passages which are predominantly harmonic:

(Mendelssohn, Concerto in g-minor, first movement)

"½ pedal" need not be released for staccato notes:

(Beethoven, Sonata quasi una fantasia, opus 27, No. 2, last movement)

but it must be changed with each change of harmony:

Un poco animato

(Liszt, Concerto in A-major)

(Brahms, Concerto in d-minor, first movement)

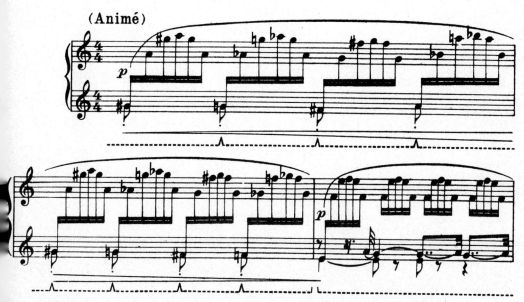

(Debussy, Le vent dans la plaine)

Published by Authorization of Durand & Cie, Publishers and Sole Owners, Paris

"½ pedal" will eliminate the impression of exaggerated shortness and dryness, often so disturbing when staccato is played without pedal:

(Beethoven, Sonata opus 14, No. 1, first movement)

(Brahms, Concerto in d-minor, 2nd movement)

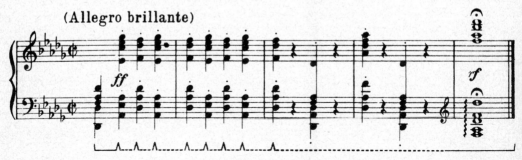

(Schumann, Etudes Symphoniques, last 5 bars)

Yet the character of the staccato can be fully retained. Hence, "½ pedal" is especially recommended for "staccato" on longer note values and in slow tempo; the notes can be played very short while the "½ pedal" is held for the full note-value.

(Beethoven, Sonata opus 2, No. 3, 2nd movement).

(Schubert, Impromptu in c-minor, opus 90, No. 1)

(Mozart, Phantasie in c-minor, K.V. 475)

Thus it is also possible to distinguish notes of different lengths when played staccato. This is shown in the following example from Chopin's Polonaise in e-flat minor:

the "½ pedal" should be released exactly on the second beat, giving the first note its correct length of one quarter (crotchet); in contrast to the following eighth notes (quavers).

When legato extends across a rest, this effect may be enhanced by "½ pedal".

(Schumann, Kinderszenen, "Der Dichter spricht"; "The Poet speaks")

At the beginning of Mozart's C-major Sonata, K.V. 545

the use of conventional pedal patterns has the following effect upon the figures in the left hand. Changing every half bar will sound like this:

changing on every beat:

pedals on 1st and 3rd beat, released on 2nd and 4th:

With the help of "½ pedal", one can avoid these distortions without being forced to play without pedal. Similarly, in the second movement of Beethoven's f-minor Sonata, opus 57,

one may wish to avoid the following impression:

or in the middle section of the first "Moment Musical" by Schubert:

where the use of "½ pedal" as marked in this example eliminates the effect of:

There are countless places where conventional use of the pedal creates the impression that notes are held.

In other places the composer seems to indicate that he wishes certain notes held and others not. Thus in Brahms' Intermezzo opus 117 No. 2 we suggest the following use of the pedal:

or in the A-major Sonata opus 120 by Schubert:

Allegro moderato

Lastly, the "½ pedal" may be useful for special effects when slight blurring is wanted:

Modérément animé

(Debussy, "La sérénade interrompue")

Published by Authorization of Durand & Cie, Publishers and Sole Owners, Paris

* * * * * *

Increasing the amount of "Nachklang" once more by lifting the dampers slightly further, we obtain an effect which is quite similar to the conventional, "full" pedal. It should give the impression that a note is held after the key is released but should differ from "full pedal" by its transparency of sound. We call this effect "*3/4 pedal*" and shall indicate its use by the following method of marking:

"¾ pedal" can produce the effect of great brilliance as its sound is both transparent and very resonant.

It seems a better choice than "full pedal" for the opening chords of Schubert's Fantasie opus 15 ("Wanderer-Fantasie"):

Allegro con fuoco ma non troppo

(for the arpeggio and the following staccati, "½ pedal" is recommended) or for this passage from the same piece:

or for the following examples:

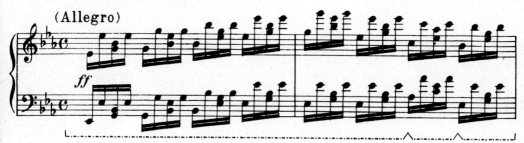

(Beethoven, Concerto in E-flat major, first movement)

Presto con fuoco

(Chopin, Ballade in F-major)

Also in p , "¾ pedal" may be preferable at times to "full" or "½ pedal":

(Andante (quasi Allegretto) consolante)

(Weber, Sonata in e-minor, 3rd movement)

(Schumann, "Aufschwung"—"Soaring")

Here, Schumann marked the top voice as quarter and eighth notes (crotchets and quavers). It would be very difficult to play this voice legato, as indicated by Schumann, if "½" or less pedal were used.

"¾ pedal" is particularly useful in all places where one or more notes are required to be held but cannot be held by means of the fingers while at the same time scales or other non-harmonic passages have to be played.

(Schumann, "Haschemann"—"Catch me if you can" from "Kinderszenen")

The "¾ pedal" will hold the bass notes as required while there will be less blurring than with the use of "full pedal."

Likewise in the "Préambule" of Schumann's "Carnaval":

In the following example from Brahms' Sonata in f-minor, opus 5

the pedal markings are original indications by the composer. However, the blurring caused by the changing harmonies will be diminished if "¾ pedal" is used instead of "full pedal".

In the second movement of the C-major Fantasie by Schumann a similar example with original pedal indications is found:

Here the ♪ -rests cannot be observed when "full pedal" is used.

* * * * * *

On pianos with 3 pedals, a better performance of the previous examples is possible by using the *middle-pedal* in the manner shown below. In the next two examples the pedal markings refer to the use of the middle-pedal, not the right pedal. The middle-pedal can *not* be used in intermediate positions; it must be fully depressed.

(Schumann, "Haschemann"—"Catch me if you can", from "Kinderszenen")

(Schumann, "Préambule", from "Carnaval")

While the middle-pedal is held down, the right pedal can be used, but it is important to watch that the right pedal is *not* in use at the moment when the middle pedal is being depressed. In the following illustrations, two lines of pedal markings are shown: the upper line refers to the right pedal (right foot), the lower line to the middle-pedal (left foot):

(Brahms, Sonata in f-minor, opus 5, Finale)

It is also possible to combine use of the middle-pedal with intermediate positions of the right pedal:

(Schumann, Fantasie in C-major, opus 17)

*   *   *   *   *   *

It should always be remembered that the terms "¼", "½" and "¾" pedal do not refer to specific positions of the pedal, nor even to specific positions of the dampers, but only to the amount of sound which remains when keys are released. The *only* way to recognize "¼", "½" and "¾" pedals, to distinguish between them or to judge whether they are performed correctly, is by *hearing* the effect created.

If one wishes to learn using "intermediate pedals", one should start by playing short notes and chords while holding the pedal in various intermediate positions and listening carefully to the different effects created.

To test whether a certain position of the pedal produces the effect of "*1/4 pedal*" accurately, play a scale or a succession of different harmonies: there should be no blurring until the last note has been played *; play the same passage again, but without pedal: there should be a marked difference in sound.

To test "*1/2 pedal*", play single staccato notes or chords: they should sound staccato; play a scale or succession of different harmonies: there should be some blurring.

To test "*3/4 pedal*", play a chord, then release the keys: it should sound as if the chord were held out; play and release the same chord again, using "full pedal": there should be a marked difference in sound.

Learning to produce the desired effect immediately should not take much time, if the same piano is always used. Changing from one piano to another, one has to compensate for the difference between the pedals of the various pianos. To be able to do this automatically and almost instantly requires considerable experience. No amount of experience can enable a pianist, playing on a certain piano for the first time, to predict what effect he will obtain when using the first "intermediate pedal"; but this applies as well to dynamics: it is also impossible to predict how loud the first tone will sound.

*   *   *   *   *   *

(*If the pedal is kept in this position *after* the last note has been played, a slight blurring might be audible.)

Many special effects can be created by changing directly from one intermediate position to another, or between intermediate and "full pedals." A few of these are illustrated in the subsequent paragraphs.

A rapid diminuendo in a harmonic passage can be achieved by releasing the pedal gradually, thereby passing all intermediate positions:

(Schubert, Sonata in a-minor, opus 143, last movement)

The effect of " *fp* " on a single note or chord:

(Beethoven, Sonate Pathétique opus 13, opening chords)

(Schubert, Sonata in B-flat major, opus posth., first movement)

(Schubert, Moment Musical. No. 6)

Allegro ma non troppo

(Schubert, Sonata in B-flat major, opus posth., last movement)

can be obtained by means of the pedal. There are three different methods, making it possible to vary the degree and suddenness of dynamic decrease considerably. For a very slight decrease it is recommended to change the pedal while the keys remain fully depressed:

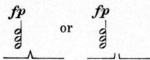

For a more marked decrease, the pedal should be changed while the keys are partially released (i.e., the keys are lifted for a very small part of the total height of the key-motion).

If a violent decrease of tone is desired, the keys should be entirely released while the pedal is fully depressed and then the pedal should be partially released and immediately depressed again (i.e., the pedal should be changed from "full pedal" to an intermediate position and back to "full pedal"). Here the degree of decrease will depend upon the speed with which this partial pedal-change is executed and upon the position to which the pedal is lifted during the change.

In all three methods, the pedal change can be performed immediately after the beat or later, offering further possibilities for varying the effect.

It is somewhat more difficult but most effective to combine the second and third methods: changing the pedal partially while the keys are partially released.

If the keys are kept in this position while the partial change of the pedal is repeated continuously, a gradual decrease of tone can be achieved. The motion should be similar to that of "vibrating pedal", but it should alternate between "full pedal" and an intermediate position, not between "full pedal" and "no pedal," as for the "vibrating pedal" effect. In the following examples the indications of the composer seem to require an effect of this kind:

Presto con fuoco

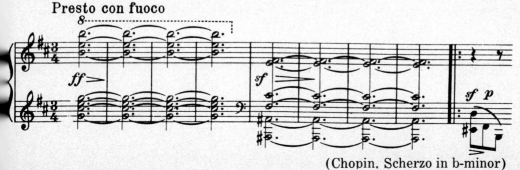

(Chopin, Scherzo in b-minor)

(Chopin, Scherzo in c-sharp minor)

(Schubert, Sonata in a-minor, opus 143, first movement)

There will always be a decrease of tone, of course, when a note or chord is held—by fingers or pedal—even without using any special technique. But the listener is accustomed to this decrease of tone which he hears with every note played on a piano and therefore it does not give him the impression of being a diminuendo. Only a more rapid decrease of tone, as it can be obtained by the method described above, will give that impression.

* * * * * *

Partial changes of pedal can be useful in many other instances; they are applicable wherever it is desired to retain some but not all of the preceding sound.

We shall use the following symbol to indicate a partial pedal change: ____·____ the dot marks the instant when the pedal should be partially released.

(Mässig. Durchaus energisch)

(Schumann, Fantasie in C-major)

(Brahms, Rhapsody in g-minor)

Also at a change of harmony the effect created by a partial pedal change may be desirable, as for instance in the first bar of Debussy's "Les Sons et les parfums tournent dans l'air du soir": (by permission Durand & Cie)

In another example from the same piece, a partial change on the fourth beat and a partial or complete change on the fifth beat are recommended:

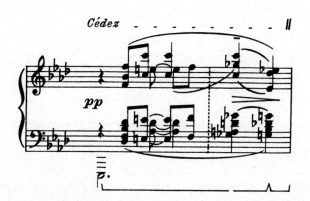

The use of partial changes throughout the first movement of the "Sonata quasi una fantasia" opus 27, No. 2, by Beethoven may be the best solution.

(Adagio sostenuto)

Two indications by *Beethoven* refer to the use of the pedal in this piece: "Si deve suonare tutto questo pezzo delicatissimamente e *senza sordino*" and "sempre *pp* e *senza sordino*". In many other instances, when Beethoven uses the expression "senza sordino" ("without dampers") it is followed by "con sordino". It is generally agreed that this has the following meaning: at the indication "senza sordino" the pedal should be depressed and should stay depressed until the indication "con sordino" appears, when it should be released.

Many of *Beethoven's* pedal markings indicate that the pedal should be held down during changes of harmonies. We believe that in most of these places the best realization can be achieved by using "full pedal," without any change, for the total duration of Beethoven's pedal marking. However, if this cannot be carried out successfully, it should be helpful to use "partial changes", as this will certainly produce better results than complete pedal changes.

Schumann marks "Pedale" or " 𝓟𝓮𝓭." at the beginning of many of his pieces or sections of pieces. Obviously this refers to the general use of pedal throughout such pieces or sections, meaning that the pedal should be depressed, changed and released in the appropriate places. In some cases, as for instance the 8th piece of "Kreisleriana":

Schnell und spielend

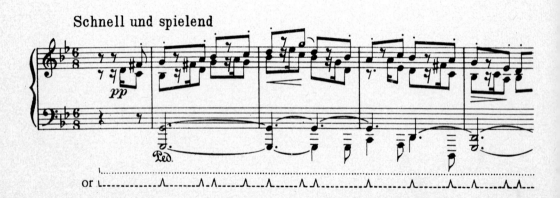

or the 4th Variation from "Etudes Symphoniques"

any use of "full pedal" seems contrary to other indications by the composer (staccati, pauses) while intermediate pedals seem ideally suited.

The use of the pedal is indicated in great detail by *Chopin*. Yet, also in his works there are numerous instances where the pedal marks seem to contradict or cancel other indications by the composer:

(Chopin, Scherzo in b-flat minor)

"Full pedal" creates the following impression:

This is obviously not what Chopin intended. Releasing the pedal on the second beat produces an unsatisfactory result, which explains the necessity of Chopin's pedal marking.

The best solution seems "½ pedal"

Similarly, the original pedal indications in bars 18-19

and the last 9 bars of the same composition are significant.

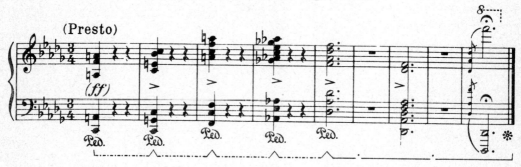

At the beginning of the E-major Scherzo, pedal markings appear mainly in those bars where they seem to contradict other indications:

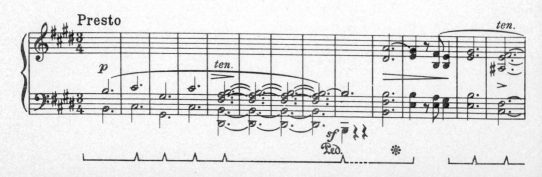

while later in the same piece

considerable blurring would result, if the pedal marking were executed with "full pedal."

In the first 2 bars of the A-major Polonaise

use of "full pedal" would make the different notation of the first bar (pauses, not legato) and second bar (no pause, legato) superfluous; pauses and staccati would be cancelled in bars 10 - 13 of the Polonaise in A-flat major:

likewise in the "Barcarole"

where it would also cause intense blurring, especially if the diminuendo is properly executed.

In all the above examples, recommended "intermediate pedals" are marked below Chopin's pedal indications. The examples were selected at random; there are many more and possibly better examples in Chopin's works.

We consider it not at all impossible that Chopin as well as Schumann intended to indicate the use of intermediate pedals in some or all of these instances; but, of course, no means of indication existed.

We shall conclude our recommendations with a summary of all the symbols used in our suggested method of pedal-markings:

Conventional, "full pedal" : ⌞____⌟ ⌞_⌟ ⌞_ΛΛΛ_⌟ ⌞_Λ_⌟ ⌞_ᴧ_⌟

    "¼ pedal" : ⌞...⌟

    "½ pedal" : ⌞-------⌟ ⌞---⌟ ⌞_ΛΛΛΛ--⌟ ⌞_Λ-⌟ ⌞_ᴧ_⌟

    "¾ pedal" : ⌞.-...-.⌟ ⌞-_-⌟ ⌞_Λ.Λ.Λ.Λ__⌟ ⌞_Λ.⌟ ⌞._ᴧ_⌟

    complete pedal change : fast: ─Λ─ ;   slower: ──ᴧ──

    partial change :   ____.____

    "vibrating pedal" :   wwwwwwww

Ludwig van BEETHOVEN

Edited by ARTHUR SCHNABEL

32 SONATAS

4279   Volume   I (1-12)

4280   Volume II (13-23)

4281   Volume III (24-32)

Trilingual edition: either Italian, English and German, or Italian, French, and Spanish

Franz SCHUBERT

Edited by KARL ULRICH SCHNABEL

4976   ## GRAN DUO Op. 140

In Italian, English, French, and German

5129   ## SONATA Op. 120

Trilingual edition: Italian, English, and French

4977   ## 20 DANCES

In Italian, English, French, and German

Carl Maria von WEBER

Edited by KARL ULRICH SCHNABEL

5130   ## 5 PIECES (for Two Pianos)